ABBEY COTTAGE

Home & Hearty

COOKBOOK

ACKNOWLEDGEMENTS

To all the Abbey Cottage Staff who over the past 30 years have worked with us and contributed so much to our success.

To our family, friends and neighbours who have encouraged and supported us, by sharing recipes, donating fruit and vegetable surpluses, and in many other ways.

Thank you Shona. With us from the beginning, and our biggest supporter.

Published by Frozen World Publishing, November 2013.

Illustrations by Val Macadam

Design by weesleekit

ISBN 978-0-9571056-1-4

Foreword

After years of friends and family telling us that opening a tearoom at Abbey Cottage was the thing to do, we did it. That was in 1983.

We had no idea then that our little venture would grow into the family business it is today.

So, when our friends, family and customers started asking us for a recipe book, we listened!

Over the years we have gathered many, many recipes. Some of them are family recipes that have come from old recipe notebooks tucked in kitchen drawers, some scribbled on bits of paper and handed over by friends and some torn out of magazines or newspapers and given a tweak here or there.

Whatever the source, they're recipes from our homes that we've brought to Abbey Cottage. We've chosen some that we think you'll enjoy trying out. Nothing too fancy, just traditional home and hearty food!

Best wishes,

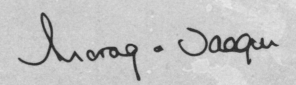

C   CARROT & COURGETTE SOUP

1 oz BUTTER
1½ lb. CARROTS
1½ lb COURGETTES

3 PINTS CHICKEN STOCK
3 BAY LEAVES
3 TABLESPOONS TOMATO PUREE
3 TABLESPOONS ...

Contents

Abbey Cottage
~A History

Max, New Abbey Secondary School

90 YEARS IN THE FAMILY

Abbey Cottage is prominently located next to the magnificent Sweetheart Abbey and must have created quite an impact when it was first built back in the 1860s. Its distinctive solid granite and sandstone Victorian architecture would have stood out from the much older houses on the village's Main Street.

In fact, it was built on glebe land, land owned by the church, as a retirement home for the housekeeper to the Minister from Kirkbean parish.

It has been part of our family for more than 90 years. It was acquired by Auntie Moshie, who was an infant school mistress. It was to be her retirement home. Although none of the current family ever lived in Abbey Cottage, we've always known the village, and some of us even went to Secondary School in New Abbey!

Since Auntie Moshie's time, Abbey Cottage has been a family home, a holiday home and, for the past 30 years, a tearoom.

Lesley & Jacqui in new tearoom with flowers by Lindsay

Abbey Cottage Coffees

Homemade soup & granary bread   35p.
Salads & granary bread :-
Roast beef -
Egg mayonnaise -   2·25p.
Ploughman's lunch -   1·95p.
Galloway Country paté &
Baked potato & side salad
Plain with butter
Tuna & onion ~
Cheese ~
Cheese with onion ~
Cheese with pickle ~
Egg mayonnaise

Thank you for not smoking

Shona, Jacqui, Morag and Fiona, April 2013

The original team. Fiona, Jacqui, Anne and Lesley

1983

Abbey Cottage Coffees

Soup of the day   35p
Selection of sandwiches   55p.
Toasties   65p

Danish open sandwiches:
Prawn   1·50p
Garlic sausage   1·20p
Paté salad & toast   1·20p
Ploughmans lunch   1·20p

Icecream   35p
Fruit tart   50p
Cheesecake   60
Gâteau   65
Scone & butter   2
Fruit loaf & butter
Selection of home baking   8p
Chocolate biscuits   15p.

30p

Coffee   20p

8

Abbey Cottage ~A Family Business

BEGINNINGS: OPENING THE DOOR

Things were a lot different at Abbey Cottage when we made our first batch of scones in 1983! With only a few changes to the original building, we carefully wrote the menus by hand and opened for business with crockery from Habitat, and some home made tablecloths and curtains made with Laura Ashley fabric.

From that moment the story of Abbey Cottage has been a whole family project. Our first waitresses were Jacqui and Lesley McKie and two of their friends Anne and Fiona. Every generation of the family were involved too. Grandparents helped out by baking tarts and making pancakes before calling in to give the girls 'a wee hand' or tending the garden and cutting the grass in return for tea and a scone!

The original Abbey Cottage home was unchanged. The tearoom was the living room with tables and chairs for 20 people. The kitchen was entirely original and visitors to our bathroom found everything they'd expect including the bath!

Starting up had been something of a step into the dark. We weren't sure if we would be successful and were unsure if we could even make a living. However by the end of that first year we had a mention in the Egon Ronay 'Just a Bite' guide book, which suggested we must have been doing something right! So we kept on opening the doors and carried on.

Lesley, Sally and Shona. Abbey Cottage garden

After those early days, it soon became clear the tearoom needed to be bigger. On busy days people were queuing outside and the kitchen was simply too small a space. So in 1991 the builders started work, adding the new tearoom at the rear of Abbey Cottage. The new space makes the most of the lovely view across to the ruins of Sweetheart Abbey. With French windows opening onto the patio garden customers can even enjoy eating out. For the staff, the extension gave them a larger, modern kitchen. Finally, the old bathroom was ripped out and replaced with 'proper loos'.

Max lifting onions

GARDENING AND GROWING OUR OWN

As a family we've always had a vegetable garden and fruit bushes. So, from the beginning, seasonal produce has made its way to the Abbey Cottage kitchen. Our menu makes the most of a regular and plentiful supply of salad leaves and herbs. Leeks, kale, potatoes, carrots and courgettes all make their way into our soups. And our home grown black currants, raspberries and strawberries are in demand for jams, crumbles and tarts. Of course, working with fresh produce does occasionally come with a surprise in the kitchen as a frog pops out of the leaves looking a little confused before being swiftly re-homed in the garden. Even the greengage tree in the garden at Abbey Cottage produces fruit for the kitchen in good years. And we continue to be amazed at how much jam our customers eat. Each year we make 250 jars of jam!

Thirty years on, Max is still in charge of the garden, and has expanded his production to a polytunnel. He can now extend the growing season and produce more salad leaves in the Spring and Autumn. As one of the unsung heroes of our story, he's always looking for willing helpers, and any available grandchild will get a wee job to do.

WORKING WITH LOCAL PRODUCERS

Making the most of the produce we had to hand got us through the early years, but now we need to use lots of different suppliers. We make a point of carefully choosing local producers for most of our ingredients. Dumfries and Galloway has some amazing food producers, and we enjoy working with them and presenting their foods and incorporating their flavours into our dishes. It is all part of being rooted in the region. In days gone by we had a local man calling in to tell us he was going fishing that day, only to drop off a salmon for the kitchen later on. Our waitresses have been known to arrive with their arms straining under boxes of strawberries from their gardens. You can't get much fresher or more local than that!

OUR CUSTOMERS

It would have been impossible in the early days to stay open year round. Today we are open for eleven months of the year, but we still close for a month to re-charge our batteries. We have loyal and supportive customers. Local people and visitors alike return again and again. As they have spread the word about our baking and cooking, we have expanded to provide Christmas lunches, cater for private parties for walking or cycling groups and local societies. We have even provided impromptu wedding breakfasts for couples before their nuptials in Sweetheart Abbey, and kept visiting film crews well fed after a long morning on location.

WINNERS

Along the way we have picked up awards for our menu, service and our commitment to good produce. The UK Tea Council has consistently awarded us for our presentation of quality tea. But, without doubt, the highest accolade we have achieved is the Macallan Taste of Scotland award. We beat off competition from across the country for the honour of dressing up in our finest to collect the award at a glittering ceremony in Glasgow. In collecting it, we felt it was for everyone in the region who supplies, for our staff who prepare and serve and for Dumfries and Galloway, an all too often overlooked corner of the world.

30 YEARS IN BUSINESS

It hardly seems to have been so long, but we have been baking scones and serving our customers for over thirty years. What began as a multi generation family enterprise is still that today, with three generations of our own family involved!

In the eighties, the expectation from a tearoom menu was fairly conservative. All our tastes have changed since then and we have continued to evolve and change, moving with the times and the demands of our customers. Abbey Cottage now has a broad menu of speciality teas. We make smoothies, and we have enjoyed seeing the revival of afternoon teas. But whatever the trends in catering, throughout our thirty years we have remained true to our original ethos: home baking, and homely and hearty food.

Left; Jacqui and Morag. Macallan Taste of Scotland Award

Papa and a wee helper (Stephanie)

RECIPES

Soups Jams SNACKS

Afternoon Tea

CAKES & PUDS

COOKING WITH KIDS

Seasonal Treats

...AND MUCH MORE!

Abbey Cottage
Tearoom
Crafts
Gallery

30 Years

Granny recipes

HONEY

3 onions
4 carrots
2 handfuls flat leas.
2 small potatoes

Soups

POTATO AND LEEK
SOUP CAULIFLOWER
AND STILTON SOUP
SWEET POTATO AND
RED PEPPER SOUP
SPICY BROCCOLI AND
LENTIL SOUP SPICY
BUTTERNUT SQUASH
SOUP COURGETTE
AND CARROT SOUP
CURRIED PARSNIP SOUP
VEGETABLE BROTH
LENTIL SOUP

POTATO AND LEEK SOUP

serves 4 - 6

Ingredients:

4 leeks
4 potatoes
50g butter/margarine
1.2 litres vegetable stock
Salt and pepper to season
2 tablespoons single cream or
Crème Fraiche (optional)

Method:

Trim and clean the leeks. Peel the potatoes and cut into large chunks.

Put the leeks and the potatoes into food processor to chop them up. Melt the butter in a large pan and add the vegetables. Cook them gently in the melted butter for about 5 minutes or until the leeks begin to soften. Add the stock, bring to the boil, then lower the heat and simmer for 30 minutes.

For a smooth soup, remove the pan from the heat and blitz the soup with a hand blender.

Taste for seasoning, and stir in the cream before serving.

CAULIFLOWER AND STILTON SOUP

serves 4 - 6

Ingredients:

1 tablespoon veg oil
1 large cauliflower
2 onions
100g Stilton
1 litre veg stock
Salt and freshly ground pepper
2 tablespoons crème fraiche (optional)

Method:

Peel and chop the onion. Break up the cauliflower into florets.

Heat the oil in a large pan and add the onion. Cook gently for 10 minutes to soften the onion. Then add the cauliflower florets and the stock. Bring to the boil, then leave to simmer for 25 minutes.

Remove from the heat and blitz with a hand held blender.

Add the crumbled Stilton to the soup and place the pan back on a gentle heat to melt the cheese. Finally, stir through the crème fraiche.

Before serving, check if seasoning is required.

SWEET POTATO AND RED PEPPER SOUP

serves 4

A REALLY COLOURFUL SOUP!

Ingredients:

25g butter/vegetable oil
1 onion chopped
1 clove of garlic, crushed
2½ teaspoons ground coriander
450g sweet potato, peeled and chopped
2 red peppers, chopped
700ml vegetable stock
200ml coconut milk (½ a large tin) or 100g creamed coconut and an additional 200ml vegetable stock

Method:

Peel and chop the onion and crush the garlic. Put the oil in a large pan, add the onions and garlic and fry gently until they are soft.

Add the ground coriander, mixing it through the onions and garlic and cook for a further 2-3 minutes.

Add the chopped sweet potatoes and the chopped peppers and stir. Then add the vegetable stock and bring to the boil. Turn the heat down and simmer for 20 minutes.

Take the pan off the heat and allow to cool slightly, then blitz with a hand blender to make smooth soup.

To serve, stir and reheat the soup gently, adding the coconut milk (or creamed coconut).

SPICY BROCCOLI AND LENTIL SOUP

serves 4 - 6

Ingredients:

25g margarine or butter
2 heads of broccoli, trimmed
1 onion, peeled and chopped
1 potato, peeled and chopped
¼ teaspoon chilli powder
2 dessert-spoons red lentils
75g garlic and herb cream cheese
1 litre veg stock
Salt and freshly ground pepper

Method:

Melt the margarine or butter in a large pan and add the broccoli, onions and potatoes with chilli powder. Cook over a gentle heat for 5 minutes, until the onions soften.

Rinse the red lentils and add to the pan. Stir through and cook for a further two minutes. Next, add 750ml of the veg stock and bring to boil and simmer for about 20 minutes.

Check that the potatoes are soft and the lentils thoroughly cooked. Remove the pan from the heat and whiz with a hand blender. Add the remaining stock to the pan to get the desired consistency.

SPICY BUTTERNUT SQUASH SOUP

serves 8-10

Ingredients:

2 tablespoons vegetable oil
2 carrots
2 onions
1 butternut squash
200g potatoes
1 clove of garlic, crushed
¼ teaspoon chilli powder
½ tablespoon grated fresh root ginger
½ teaspoon ground cumin
1.5 litres vegetable stock
Salt and pepper

Method:

Peel and chop the vegetables, removing the seeds from the butternut squash, and crush the garlic. Put the oil in a large pan, add the onions and garlic and grated ginger and fry gently until they are soft. Next, add the chilli and cumin, stir through and cook for a further 2-3 minutes. Then, add all the remaining vegetables and the vegetable stock and bring to the boil. Turn the heat down and simmer for 20 minutes.

Take the pan off the heat and allow to cool slightly, then blitz with a hand blender to make smooth soup.

To serve, stir and reheat the soup gently and add seasoning to taste.

USES A WHOLE BUTTERNUT SQUASH - PUT SOME IN THE FREEZER!

COURGETTE AND CARROT SOUP

serves 6

Ingredients:

25g butter
750g carrots
750g courgettes
1.75 litres chicken stock
3 bay leaves
3 tablespoons tomato puree
3 tablespoons caster sugar
Salt and pepper
3 tablespoons cream (optional)

Method:

Peel and roughly chop the carrots. Chop the courgettes. If the courgettes are large the skin could be coarse, so peel them as well.

Melt the butter in a large pan and add the chopped vegetables. Cook gently for 5 10 minutes, then add the stock and the remaining items.

Leave to simmer for 30 minutes.

Allow to cool slightly, remove the bay leaves and liquidise with hand blender.

Season to taste and serve with the cream stirred through.

 TOO MANY COURGETTES IN THE GARDEN?

CURRIED PARSNIP SOUP

serves 4

A LOVELY WARMING SOUP!

Ingredients:

30ml vegetable oil
450g parsnips
1 onion, chopped
1 teaspoon curry powder
700ml vegetable stock
Salt and pepper
150ml single cream (optional)

Method:

Peel and chop the parsnips and onion. Put the oil in a large pan, add the chopped vegetables and fry gently for 10 minutes.
Add the curry powder, stir to coat all the vegetables and continue to cook for 2-3 minutes.
Add the stock and bring to the boil. Turn the heat down and simmer for 30 minutes.

Take the pan off the heat and allow to cool slightly, then blitz with a hand blender to make smooth soup.

To serve, stir and reheat the soup gently, adding the cream if required. Serve with parsley garnish and crusty bread.

VEGETABLE BROTH

serves 4-6

CHUNKY SOUP

Ingredients:

1 tablespoon veg oil
1 onion, peeled
1 potato, peeled
1 leek, cleaned and sliced
2 carrots, peeled
¼ small turnip (swede), peeled
Handful of chopped kale or spring greens
150g of broth soup mix (mixed lentils, barley, rice and split peas)
1 litre veg stock
Salt and freshly ground pepper

Method:

Place the broth soup mix in cold water and leave to soak, overnight if you have time.

When you are ready to prepare the soup, drain the soaked mix in a sieve, rinse with cold water and set to one side.

Chop the carrots, potato, turnip into small regular sized pieces. Finely chop the onion, slice the leek and chop the greens.

Heat the oil in a large pan. Add the onion and cook gently for 5 minutes to soften. Add the leek and continue to cook for a further 5 minutes. Next, add all the remaining vegetables, except the greens. Add the broth soup mix and the stock and stir. Bring to the boil, then lower the heat and simmer for 30 minutes. Add the greens and simmer for another 10-15 minutes.

Check for seasoning, adding salt and pepper if required, and serve with crusty bread for a warming lunch.

This recipe could be suitable for vegan, dairy free and gluten free diets – but do check the contents advice on the stock/bouillon and broth mix product labels.

- -

LENTIL SOUP

serves 4-6

TRADITIONAL SOUP

Ingredients:

3 onions
4 carrots
2 handfuls of yellow split peas or red lentils
2 small potatoes
2-3 ham stock cubes
Salt and pepper to taste
1.2 litres of water

Method:

Peel and chop up all the vegetables. Put the split peas into a sieve and rinse.

Place all of the ingredients into a large pot, and cover with the cold water. Bring to the boil and then simmer for an hour.

Use a hand blender to make smooth soup, and season to taste.

Lunchtime & Snacks

GALLOWAY BEEF
CASSEROLE WITH
MUSTARD CROUTONS
SMOKED BACON,
PRAWN AND CREAM
CHEESE PATE BEAN
AND HAZELNUT PATE
CORONATION CHICKEN
HERBY MONIAIVE
LAMB COBBLER CHILLI
VEGETARIAN CHILLI
CHICKEN AND LEEK PIE
HAM AND LEEK LASAGNE
TUNA CRUNCH DRESSING
FOR SALADS SHEPHERD'S
PIE HOT SMOKED SALMON
WITH CREME FRAICHE
AND HORSERADISH
RATATOUILLE HOT POT

GALLOWAY BEEF CASSEROLE WITH MUSTARD CROUTONS

serves 4

Ingredients:

750g diced Galloway Beef stewing steak
3 tablespoons oil
2 tablespoons plain flour
3 onions, sliced
1 clove garlic
100g smoked streaky bacon
200ml Criffel Ale
75ml beef stock
1 tablespoon brown sugar
2 tablespoon red wine vinegar
1 tablespoon chopped mixed herbs (parsley, thyme)
1 bay leaf
Salt and pepper

Croutons:

2 large slices white bread
2 teaspoons Galloway Mustard
2 tablespoons oil

Method:

Heat the oil in a large pan or casserole and add the meat chunks, frying a few at a time.

Remove the meat pieces onto a plate when they are browned all over. Lower the heat and add the onions and garlic to the pan. Fry gently until the onion and garlic have softened and are beginning to colour (about 5 minutes).

Add the flour to the pan and stir around, scraping the tasty cooked bits from the sides and bottom of the pan. Keep on the heat until the flour, onion and garlic mixture begins to brown. Add the Criffel Ale and the stock and bring to the boil. Then add the meat and the remaining ingredients and stir well.

The casserole will now need to cook slowly for a couple of hours until the meat is tender. It can be left on a low heat on the hob or transferred to the oven at 160°. It could also be transferred to a slow cooker, where it would require approximately 4-5 hours.

Make the croutons when you are ready to serve.

Remove the crusts from the bread and cut diagonally into triangles. Spread both sides of the bread with the mustard. Heat the oil in a frying pan and fry the croutons until they are browned on both sides. Serve the casserole with some chopped parsley garnish and the mustard croutons.

SMOKED BACON, PRAWN AND CREAM CHEESE PATE

serves 6

GREAT WITH GALLOWAY OATCAKES

Ingredients:

75g cooked shelled prawns
3 rashers of smoked bacon
200g Loch Arthur cream cheese
1 clove of garlic - finely chopped
1 tablespoon lemon juice
1 tablespoon finely chopped parsley
freshly ground black pepper

Method:

Chop the prawns. Fry the bacon until crisp and drain on kitchen paper and break into small pieces.

Beat the cream cheese until it is smooth, then add all the other ingredients to the cream cheese and mix well.

Serve with oatcakes.

BEAN AND HAZELNUT PATE

makes 4 starter portions

Ingredients:

400g kidney beans
25g ground hazelnuts
75g cream cheese
25g melted butter
2 dessert-spoons of Mango and
Ginger chutney
Salt and pepper to taste
Chopped parsley to garnish

Method:

Drain the beans.

Place all the ingredients into the bowl
of a food processor and blitz. Taste
and check for seasoning, adding salt
and pepper if required, and blitz again.

Transfer the pate to a serving dish,
or 4 small ramekins, and place in the
fridge to chill.

Garnish with chopped parsley and serve
with crusty bread, toast or Galloway
Oatcakes.

CORONATION CHICKEN

BRILLIANT FILLING FOR BAKED POTATOES, WRAPS AND SANDWICHES

Ingredients:

450g chicken breast, diced
1 tablespoon oil
1 onion
2 teaspoons curry powder
2 teaspoons tomato puree
2 tablespoons red wine
2 tablespoons chicken stock
125ml mayonnaise
2 tablespoons mango chutney

Method:

In advance:

Grill or lightly fry the chicken breasts, then
chill. Chop the onion and cook in the oil until
soft, add the curry powder, stir and cook for
a further 2-3 minutes. Then add the chicken
stock and red wine and bring to the boil.
Simmer for 5 minutes then remove from the
pan and place in a dish to chill.

To assemble:

Dice the chilled chicken breasts and place
in a bowl with the onion mixture and the
remaining ingredients (tomato puree,
mayonnaise and mango chutney). Mix
together so that the chicken pieces are coated
and the sauce has blended.
Will keep for up to 2 days in a cool fridge.

THE HEARTS IN THIS DISH DERIVE FROM THE STORY OF SWEETHEART ABBEY - NEXT DOOR TO ABBEY COTTAGE

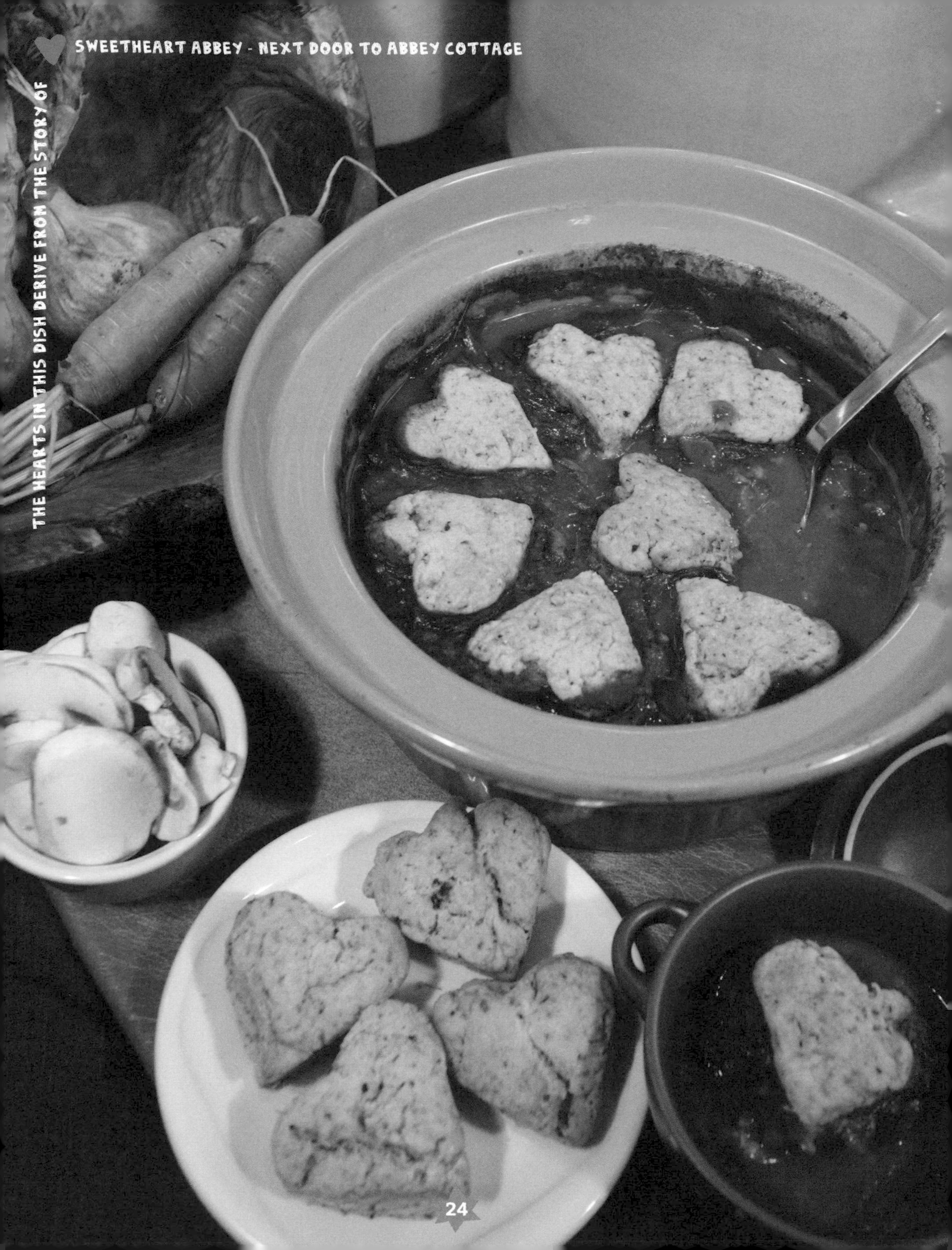

HERBY MONIAIVE LAMB COBBLER

Ingredients:

2 tablespoons olive oil
200g smoked streaky bacon chopped/lardons
900g lamb neck fillet, in large chunks
350g small onions or shallots
5 carrots
350g button mushrooms
3 tablespoons plain flour
3 bay leaves
Small bunch of fresh thyme
350ml red wine
350ml lamb or beef stock
Splash of Worcestershire Sauce

Cobbler topping:

350g self raising flour
4 tablespoons mixed chopped fresh herbs
(thyme, rosemary, parsley)
200g chilled butter
Juice of 1 lemon
5 bay leaves
1 egg beaten (to glaze)
Salt and pepper

Method:

Pre heat the oven to 180°.

Place the oil in a flameproof casserole and add the bacon, cooking until crisp. Next, add the lamb chunks and cook until brown, approximately 10 minutes.

Remove the meats and increase the heat. Add the onions, mushrooms and chopped carrots and cook for 5 minutes until the veg starts to colour. Then, stir in the flour, add the meats and herbs, then the red wine, stock and Worcestershire Sauce. Put the lid on the casserole and place in the oven for 1 hour 20 minutes.

When the lamb has been in the oven for 1 hour, start making the cobbler topping. Put the flour, herbs and seasoning into a large bowl. Add the butter (grated or chopped) and mix it well, with a fork or with your hands to make a breadcrumb consistency. Add the lemon juice and 3 tablespoons of water to a well in the centre of the mixture, and mix together to make a soft dough. Place the dough on a floured board and lightly roll it out to approximately 0.5cm thick. Cut into rounds using a pastry/scone cutter. Gather up the trimmings, mix together with your hands and re roll and cut again until all the dough is used.

After 1hr 20 minutes, carefully lift the casserole out of the oven. Remove the lid and arrange the dough rounds around the outside of the dish, overlapping each other. Stick bay leaves between them and brush with the beaten egg. Put back into the oven and back for a further 45 minutes until risen and golden.

AS WELL AS LEADING THE TEAM AT ABBEY COTTAGE, JACQUI HELPS HER BUSY SHEPHERD HUSBAND AT HOME IN MONIAIVE.

CHILLI

serves 6-8

Ingredients:

2 tablespoons veg oil
1 kg Galloway minced beef
3 onions, chopped
4 x 400g tins chopped tomatoes
3 x 400g tins kidney beans
Handful of dried mixed herbs
3 teaspoons chilli powder
3 garlic cloves, crushed
½ tube tomato puree
2 tablespoons demerara sugar
Salt and pepper to season

Method:

Heat the oil in a large pan and add the onion and garlic. Cook gently for 5-10 minutes to soften onion. Add the mince and continue to cook, stirring from time to time, until the meat is browned.

Next stir in the chilli powder and herbs. Add the tomatoes, tomato puree, sugar and kidney beans. Bring to the boil and then lower the heat and simmer for 40-50 minutes.

Check for seasoning and add salt and pepper if necessary.

VEGETARIAN CHILLI

serves 4-6

Ingredients:

2 x bags of Quorn mince
1 tablespoon veg oil
2 onions
3 x 400g tins chopped tomatoes
2 x 400g tins kidney beans
1 dessert-spoon dried mixed herbs
1½ teaspoons chilli powder
2 garlic cloves, crushed
½ tube tomato puree
1 teaspoon sugar
Salt and pepper to season

Method:

Chop the onions. Heat the oil in a large pan and add the onions and garlic and cook slowly for 5-10 minutes until the onion softens. Next, add the herbs and chilli powder and stir through. Then add the chopped tinned tomatoes, tomato puree, sugar and drained kidney beans. Stir everything together. Increase the heat and bring to the boil, then reduce the heat and allow to simmer gently for 20 minutes. Next, add the Quorn mince to the sauce, stirring it through. Allow to simmer for a further 10 minutes.

Check for seasoning before serving, adding salt and pepper if required.

CHICKEN AND LEEK PIE

Ingredients:

2 tablespoons olive oil
4 diced chicken breasts
2 leeks, finely sliced
2 carrots, chopped
450ml chicken stock
4 teaspoons Galloway wholegrain mustard
170g Loch Arthur Cream Cheese
2 teaspoons chopped tarragon
1 pack of ready rolled puff pastry

USE LEFT OVER SUNDAY ROAST!

Method:

Pre heat the oven to 180°.

Place the oil in a flameproof casserole and add the chicken pieces in 2 batches, stirring them and removing when they have browned all sides.

Next, add the leeks with a splash of water and fry them gently until soft, about 5 minutes. Then add the carrot and cook for a further 3 minutes. Then, add the stock and bring to the boil. Continue boiling until the volume of the stock has reduced by half.

While the stock is boiling, lightly grease a baking sheet and prepare the pastry. Roll out the pastry and, using a pastry cutter, create large rounds or heart shapes. Transfer them to the baking sheet.

Add the mustard and cream cheese to the pan, stirring well. Then add the chicken and tarragon and season lightly. Stir the mixture and place a tight fitting lid on the casserole.

Place the casserole and the baking sheet into the oven for 25 minutes, or until the pastry had risen and browned.

Remove from the oven, and serve with green salad or seasonal vegetables.

 WE ALWAYS HAVE LEEKS GROWING IN THE GARDEN FOR ADDING TO WINTER SOUPS AND PIES

HAM AND LEEK LASAGNE

serves 4

MAKE A MID WEEK SUPPER FROM THE WEEKEND HAM LEFTOVERS

Ingredients:

50g butter
2 leeks
225g frozen peas
350g cooked ham, chopped
6 sheets of lasagne pasta
175g of cheddar cheese, grated
75g mozzarella cheese, grated

Tomato Sauce:

400g tin of chopped tomatoes
½ tube of tomato puree
1 clove of garlic
1 tablespoon olive oil
1 dessert-spoon dried mixed herbs
2 teaspoons sugar
Salt and pepper

Béchamel Sauce:

50g flour
50g margarine
1 pint of milk
Salt and pepper

Method:

Preheat the oven to 200°. Chop the leeks and fry them gently, stirring occasionally, until they have softened (about 5 minutes). Then add the peas and the ham, stir through, and cook for a further 5 minutes. Remove from the heat and set to one side.

For the tomato sauce, finely chop the garlic and gently heat in the olive oil for 2-3 minutes. Add the tin of chopped tomatoes, the tomato puree, the mixed herbs, sugar and seasoning. Stir everything together, bring to the boil, then lower the temperature and leave the sauce to simmer for 10 minutes.

Place the lasagne sheets in a deep dish, cover with boiling water and leave them for 5 minutes.

While the lasagne is soaking, make the béchamel sauce. Melt the butter in a pan, then add the flour to form a roux. Lower the heat and gradually add the milk, stirring all the time to stop lumps from forming. Increase the heat to bring the sauce to boil to thicken, still stirring, When the sauce has thickened, remove from the heat and lightly season.

Drain the lasagne.

Place a couple of spoonfuls of the béchamel sauce on the base of the lasagne baking dish, then cover with 2 sheets of the pasta. Spread half of the leek, pea and ham mixture over the pasta sheets and scatter half of the grated cheddar over this. Then cover with the remaining béchamel sauce. Next, put on the another 2 sheets of pasta, cover with the remaining leek, pea and ham mixture, the grated cheddar and the white sauce as before. Finally, cover with the last 2 pasta sheets, pour over the tomato sauce, sprinkle with the grated mozzarella and place in the oven.

The lasagne will bake in the oven for approximately 30 minutes. It is ready when the mozzarella cheese has browned and the dish is bubbling.

Mmmmmmm.........

TUNA CRUNCH

WILL MAKE ENOUGH FOR 4 ROUNDS OF SANDWICHES, OR 2 BAKED POTATOES.

A GREAT FILLING FOR SANDWICHES, BAKED POTATO OR PANINIS.

Ingredients:

200g tuna in brine
½ red onion
1 stick celery
2 dessert-spoons Loch Arthur cream cheese
1 to 2 dessert-spoons of mayonnaise
Salt and pepper to season

Method:

Drain the tuna. Transfer to a mixing bowl and break up with a fork.

Finely chop the onion and the celery and add to the tuna. Now add the cream cheese and 1 spoonful of mayonnaise. Stir thoroughly to mix all the ingredients. Check for seasoning, and add more mayonnaise to get the desired consistency.

. . . .

 YUMMY SALAD DAYS...

DRESSING FOR SALADS

We're often complimented on our salad dressing, so here's how we make it...

250ml olive oil
250ml white wine vinegar
2 dessert-spoons caster sugar
3 dessert-spoons, Galloway grain mustard

...then you just mix everything together!

SHEPHERD'S PIE

serves 4

A FAVOURITE LUNCH OR SUPPER DISH

Ingredients:

450g minced Scottish Lamb
1 large onion, finely chopped
1 large carrot, diced
1 fresh sprig of rosemary with the leaves removed and chopped
1 large glass of red wine
400g tin chopped tomatoes
1 kg of large floury potatoes, peeled
50g butter
50g grated Scottish Cheddar
Salt and pepper

Method:

Brown the minced lamb in a large pan, stirring to break up any lumps.

Remove the mince and add the onion and rosemary to the pan. Add extra oil if necessary. Cook for 5 minutes on a medium heat, then add the carrot and cook for a further 5 minutes, until the onion is soft.

Return the mince to the pan, and with the heat still high, add the red wine. Stir to loosen the crispy bits on the bottom of the pan. Leave to bubble until half the wine has evaporated. Stir in the tinned tomatoes and leave to simmer uncovered for approximately 20 minutes.

While the sauce is simmering, cut the potatoes into large chunks and boil in lightly salted water for 10-12 minutes until very tender. Drain, and mash with the butter and half the cheese.

Check the meat sauce for seasoning, and add salt and pepper if needed. Next, spoon the meat sauce into a medium-sized oven proof dish, top with the mash, sprinkle with the remaining cheese and season with black pepper.

For immediate use, put under a pre-heated grill for 2-3 min until brown on top.

Or, reheat later in the oven at 200°C for 25-30 min.

HOT SMOKED SALMON WITH CREME FRAICHE AND HORSERADISH

A LUXURY SANDWICH FILLING

Ingredients:

200g Scottish hot smoked salmon
6 heaped dessert-spoons of crème fraiche
3 level dessert-spoons of horseradish sauce

Method:

Flake salmon into a bowl. Mix the crème fraiche and horseradish together in a bowl and then add to the salmon.

RATATOUILLE HOT POT

A TRADITIONAL VEGETABLE RATATOUILLE, WITH A WARMING POTATO AND CHEESE TOPPING. A GREAT WAY TO USE ALL THOSE HOME-GROWN COURGETTES! CAN BE MADE AS ONE BIG DISH SERVING 4-6 PEOPLE, OR IN INDIVIDUAL SERVING DISHES.

serves 4-6

Ingredients:

1 tablespoon vegetable oil
2 red onions, finely chopped
2 garlic cloves
2 red peppers, finely chopped
3 courgettes, diced
1 aubergine, diced
400g tin of chopped tomatoes
3 potatoes thinly sliced
½ teaspoon grated nutmeg
150 ml double cream
Small bunch of fresh basil, chopped
85g grated Galloway Cheddar
Salt and pepper

Method:

Pre heat the oven to 180º.

Place the oil in a flameproof casserole and add the onions. Cook on a medium heat for a couple of minutes, then add the crushed garlic, peppers, courgettes and aubergine. Continue to cook over a medium heat for another 10 minutes, until the vegetables are soft.

Add the tinned tomatoes, 4 tablespoons of water, basil and seasoning. Bring to the boil, then lower the heat, cover and leave to simmer for 15 minutes.

Place the potato slices into a bowl and season with salt, pepper and nutmeg. Pour over the cream and toss everything, making sure that all the potato slices are coated.

Take the casserole dish off the heat and remove the lid. Lay the potato slices on top of the ratatouille in a spiral pattern, then pour any remaining cream mixture over.

Place the casserole in the oven for 40 minutes. Then, remove the dish and scatter the grated Galloway cheese over the top. Put back in the oven for another 20minutes until golden brown and bubbling.

Afternoon Tea

SCONES CARROT CAKE
CHOCOLATE MINT
BAR CHURCHILL CAKE
TABLET SULTANA
FUDGE DATE LOAF
STICKY LEMON CAKE
PARKIN BISCUITS
FROSTED APRICOT,
CHERRY AND WALNUT
SLICE DATE SLICE
CUSTARD CRISPIES
GYPSY CREAMS
NAMELESS WONDERS
BRIDE'S SLICE BANANA
LOAF

SERVE WITH BUTTER, HOMEMADE JAM & CREAM (FOR A REAL TREAT!)

SCONES

EVERY MORNING WE MAKE A BATCH OF SCONES, SOME WITH FRUIT. HERE'S OUR RECIPE....

THESE QUANTITIES WILL MAKE APPROXIMATELY 8 SCONES USING A MEDIUM SIZE CUTTER.

Ingredients:

450g Self Raising Flour
100g butter (softened slightly)
80g caster sugar
½ teaspoons baking powder
150ml milk
2 large eggs

Method:

Preheat the oven to 180º.
Lightly grease and flour a large baking sheet.

First, combine the flour and butter until mixture resembles wet sand. Then, add baking powder and sugar and mix. Add sultanas at this stage if making fruit scones.

Combine the milk and eggs, and gradually add to the mixture until the dough comes together.

Gently roll out the dough and cut rounds.

LARGE HANDFUL OF SULTANAS IF MAKING FRUIT SCONES

Gather up the dough remnants and roll out and cut again until all the dough is used.

Bake for 13 to 15 minutes. Remove from the oven and cool.

CARROT CAKE

CARROT CAKE HAS ALWAYS BEEN POPULAR AT ABBEY COTTAGE, AND OUR RECIPE WAS ORIGINALLY GIVEN TO MORAG BY LIZ, WIFE OF OUR VILLAGE POLICEMAN.

Ingredients:

3 cups grated carrot
2 cups caster sugar
4 eggs
2 cups plain flour
2 teaspoons bicarbonate of soda
1½ cups of sunflower oil
2 teaspoons salt
1 teaspoon cinnamon
1 teaspoon vanilla essence
1 cup chopped nuts
1 cup raisins

Method:

Pre heat the oven to 180º. Lightly grease and line the bases of 2 large (23cm) springform cake tins.

Mix all the ingredients together, and then tip into the tins and bake for 45 mins.

While the cake is cooking, make the topping by mixing together:
25g butter
250g icing sugar
100g cream cheese

Allow the cakes to cool. Remove from the tins, spread one cake with the half the topping, place the second cake on top and cover with the remaining topping.

CHOCOLATE MINT BAR

THIS IS ONE OF THE FIRST TRAY BAKES WHICH WE SERVED AT ABBEY COTTAGE, AND IT'S STILL A FAVOURITE!

Ingredients:

200g margarine
200g Self Raising flour
150g soft brown sugar
5 good handfuls of crushed cornflakes
300g icing sugar
½ teaspoon peppermint essence
Drop of green colouring
A little water.

300g dark chocolate cake covering

 HANDY HINT: FOR LEVEL CHOCOLATE TOPPING, SHAKE THE TIN GENTLY AND TIP FROM SIDE TO SIDE BEFORE THE CHOCOLATE SETS

Method:

Lightly grease a swiss roll tin (31 x 21 cm approximately). Preheat the oven to 180°.

First make the base by melting the margarine and mix in the remaining ingredients (flour, soft brown sugar and cornflakes). Tip the mixture into the swiss roll tin, press into the corners, and level with the back of a spoon. Place in the oven and cook for 20 minutes.

Remove from the oven and set aside to cool.

To make the icing, place the icing sugar in a bowl. Add the peppermint essence and a tiny drop of green food colouring. Stir the sugar and cautiously add water, a teaspoonful at a time, until a smooth, firm and spreadable consistency is reached. Cover the cooled base with the icing.

Allow the icing to set, and cover with the melted chocolate.

Cut into squares with a sharp knife and store in a tin.

· ·

CHURCHILL CAKE

Ingredients:

100g margarine
100g caster sugar
75g plain flour
75g self raising flour
250g sultanas
100g glacé cherries
2 eggs
25g ground almonds
¼ cup of milk (approximately)

 A LOVELY PALE CAKE FULL OF FRUIT!

Method:

Pre heat the oven to 160°. Grease and line a 2lb loaf tin.

Soften margarine and cream with the sugar, then mix in all the other ingredients except the fruit. Gently stir in the sultanas and cherries and carefully transfer the mixture to the loaf tin.

Place in the centre of the oven and bake for approximately 1¼ hours.

TABLET

THIS WAS ALWAYS A HALLOWE'EN TREAT, BUT IT'S SO YUMMY THAT WE EAT IT YEAR ROUND!

Ingredients:

300ml milk
450g granulated sugar
100g butter
Few drops vanilla essence

Method:

Grease and line a 18cm tray.

Put the milk and sugar into a large pan and heat slowly until the sugar has dissolved. Do not allow to boil during this time as it will crystallise.

 A REAL TREAT IF YOU'RE LACTOSE INTOLERANT – JUST USE DAIRY FREE SPREAD AND MILK. DELICIOUS!

Then, bring to the boil and keep boiling rapidly until the mixture forms a small ball when dropped into cold water. This could take 20 minutes.

Next, take the pan off the heat and add the butter and vanilla essence and beat rapidly until the butter has melted and the mixture is beginning to set.

Tip the mixture into the tray and leave to cool. When it has set, cut into small squares and store in a tin.

SULTANA FUDGE

Ingredients:

A QUICK AND EASY TRAYBAKE!

100g butter/margarine
100g cooking chocolate
250g digestive biscuits
½ tin/200ml sweetened condensed milk
100g sultanas
Chocolate to cover

Method:

Lightly grease a baking tray of approximately 20 x 30 cm.

Crush the digestive biscuits and place in a mixing bowl with sultanas and condensed milk.

Place the chocolate and butter in a bowl and melt them together, either over a pan of hot water, or using a microwave. Be careful not to overdo it!

Add the melted chocolate and butter to the other ingredients and mix thoroughly.

Spread the mixture into the baking tray, pressing into the corners and smoothing down with the back of a spoon.

Cover with chocolate and place in the fridge to set (a couple of hours). Then, using a sharp knife, cut into portions and serve.

DATE LOAF

Ingredients:

250g cooking dates
225ml boiling water
250g self raising flour
75g sugar
1 level teaspoon bicarbonate of soda

 DON'T BURN YOUR CAKES. EVERY OVEN IS DIFFERENT. CHECK YOUR CAKE REGULARLY!

Method:

Preheat the oven to 170°. Grease and line a 2lb loaf tin.

Chop the dates and soak in the boiling water for 10 minutes. Sieve the dry ingredients into a bowl. Add the date mixture and mix well, adding a little extra water if required to make a soft dropping consistency.

Place the mixture into the loaf tin and bake for approximately 1 hour.

Serve sliced and spread with butter.

· ·

STICKY LEMON CAKE

THIS DELICIOUS LEMON DRIZZLE CAKE IS GLUTEN FREE, AND HAS A VERY SURPRISING INGREDIENT!

Ingredients:

150g unsalted butter softened
200g caster sugar
4 large eggs
225g ground almonds
2 teaspoons gluten-free baking powder
250g cold mashed potato
Finely grated zest 2 lemons
Juice of 1 lemon
Icing sugar to dust

For the syrup:

Juice 2 lemons and zest 1
5 tablespoons caster sugar

Method:

Pre heat oven to 180°.
Lightly butter the base and sides of a 23cm round springform tin and line the base with baking parchment.

Whisk together the butter and sugar until pale and fluffy. Gradually beat in the eggs, adding 1 tablespoon of ground almonds with each egg to prevent curdling. Now fold in the baking powder and remaining ground almonds. Finally, fold in the mashed potato, lemon zest and juice. Put the mixture into the prepared tin and cook in the centre of the oven for 35 to 45 minutes.

While the cake is in the oven, make the syrup. Put the lemon juice and zest and the caster sugar in a small pan and simmer gently for 1 minute.

Remove the cake from the oven, prick the surface all over with a skewer and spoon over the hot syrup until it is all absorbed. Allow the cake to cool in the tin for 1 hour before turning out to cool completely. Dust with icing sugar to serve.

PARKIN BISCUITS

makes approx 30 biscuits

Ingredients:

300g self raising flour
150g butter/margarine
150g caster sugar
1 teaspoon baking soda
2 tablespoons golden syrup

GREAT HOMEMADE BISCUITS FOR DUNKING IN TEA!

Method:

Pre heat the oven to 200° and lightly grease 2 baking sheets.

Cream the butter and sugar, then add the golden syrup and mix thoroughly.
Add the baking soda to the flour and mix, then add the flour mixture to the rest of the ingredients.

Stir the ingredients together. It will look impossible, but everything will mix into a dough!

Using your hands, roll the mixture into small balls (this recipe will make approximately 30) and space them out evenly on the baking sheets.

Bake in the oven for 15 minutes then remove and allow to cool.

FROSTED APRICOT, CHERRY AND WALNUT SLICE

Ingredients:

200g digestive biscuits
1 cup of glacé cherries
⅔ cup of chopped dried apricots
¾ cup of chopped walnuts
½ cup of desiccated coconut
½ tin of sweetened condensed milk
100g butter

Topping:

25g butter
1 teaspoon vanilla essence
2 cups icing sugar
Water to mix
Desiccated coconut to sprinkle

Method:

Lightly grease a baking tray (approximately 20cm x 30cm)

Melt the butter, crush the digestive biscuits, and halve the glacé cherries. Place all the ingredients into a large bowl and stir until everything is well mixed.

Tip the mixture into the baking tray and press it out across the tray, and level the top. The back of a spoon is useful!

Prepare the frosting topping by combining the butter, icing sugar and vanilla essence. If required, add water a drop or two at a time and keep mixing.

Spread the frosting over the mixture in the tray and then put the tray in the fridge to set. Sprinkle with coconut and cut into slices.

DATE SLICE

GREAT FOR LUNCH BOXES!

Ingredients:

200g plain flour
200g butter/margarine (in small cubes)
100g caster sugar
150g rolled (porridge) oats
1 packet (about 375g) dates
4 tablespoons water
1 tablespoon honey
1 tablespoon lemon juice

Method:

Lightly grease a baking tray (20 x 30cm approximately). Preheat the oven to 160°C.

Place the dates, water, honey and lemon juice in a bowl, separating the dates if necessary. Cook in a microwave oven for approximately 2½ minutes until the dates are soft, stopping and stirring after a minute or so. Mash lightly with a potato masher and set to the side.

Place all the other ingredients into a bowl and mix together to create a crumble-like mixture. Put half of this mixture into the tray and press it out into the corners, making a smooth surface. Now cover with the date mixture, spreading it out evenly. Finally, cover with the remaining 'crumble' mixture.

Place in the oven for 30 minutes. Remove, leave to cool then cut into slices.

CUSTARD CRISPIES

Ingredients:

Biscuits:
150g Self Raising flour
50g custard powder
50g caster sugar
150g butter/margarine
50g caster sugar (for rolling)

Filling:
50g butter
1 cup icing sugar
2 tablespoons custard powder
A drop or two of vanilla essence

THIS RECIPE WAS GIVEN TO MORAG'S MOTHER BY A COUSIN IN 1953!

Method:

Pre heat the oven to 180° and lightly grease 2 baking sheets. Cream the butter and sugar. Add the custard powder to the flour and mix, then add the flour mixture to the rest of the ingredients. Knead the ingredients together. It will look impossible, but everything will mix into a dough!

Using your hands, roll the mixture into small balls. This recipe will make approximately 24 individual biscuits; just remember that you need an even number. Roll the balls in the caster sugar and space them out evenly on the baking sheets.

Bake in the oven for 15 minutes then remove and allow to cool. To avoid the biscuits sticking to the tray, lift and move them to a cooling rack.

While the biscuits are cooking, make the filling by combining all the ingredients and mixing with the back of a fork until a creamy icing is formed.

Assemble the biscuits when completely cooled and serve that day. Delicious!

GYPSY CREAMS

THIS IS ANOTHER FAVOURITE RECIPE, AND ONE THAT LOTS OF OUR CUSTOMERS REMEMBER FROM THEIR CHILDHOODS.

makes 12

Ingredients:

Biscuits:
1 cup porridge oats
1 cup Self Raising Flour
100g butter/margarine
1 teaspoon golden syrup
½ teaspoon vanilla essence
½ teaspoon baking powder
3 teaspoons water
75g caster sugar

Icing:
50g butter/margarine
100g icing sugar
1 teaspoon cocoa

 KEEP YOUR BISCUITS FRESH AND CRISPY IN A TIN. PUT THE ICING IN THE FRIDGE. PUT THEM TOGETHER FOR A TREAT!

Method:

Pre heat the oven to 180°C. Lightly grease a large baking sheet.

To make the biscuits, cream together the butter and sugar until light and fluffy. Then, add the water and syrup, stir through and add the remaining ingredients. Stir everything together – you will have a stiff, crumbly dough. Using your hands, make the dough into an even number of balls (approximately 24), space them out on the baking sheet and press the tops lightly with the back of a fork to flatten them slighty.

Bake in the oven for 15 minutes. Bring out of the oven and set aside to cool.

The make the icing, cut the butter into small pieces and place in a bowl with the icing sugar and cocoa. Using a fork, flatten the butter into the sugar mixture until a creamy icing is formed.

Sandwich the biscuits together with the icing to serve. If left un iced, the biscuits will stay crisp in an airtight container, so we recommend just icing as you plan to use them.

NAMELESS WONDERS

A VERY YUMMY TRAY BAKE WITH A NUTTY BASE AND CUSTARD FILLING!

Ingredients:

Base:
50g mixed nuts
125g margarine
150g caster sugar
1 teaspoon vanilla essence
25g coconut
1 egg
350g digestive biscuits
1 tablespoon cocoa

Topping:
60g margarine
250g icing sugar
2 dessert-spoons custard powder
4 dessert-spoons of water
300g dark cooking chocolate to cover.

Method:

Base:
Melt the margarine, sugar and cocoa in a pan. Crush the digestive biscuits. Mix all the ingredients in a bowl, then place in the microwave for 1 minute. Press into a swiss roll tin (approximately 31cm x 21cm)

Topping:
Mix all the ingredients together. If you can, use a food processor as this stops the icing sugar flying everywhere! Spread the icing mixture over the base, leaving a smooth surface.

Melt the chocolate and spread over.
Leave to set, then cut into 16 or 20 portions.

(handwritten note:)
BRIDES SLICE
Line tin with shortcrust pastry
(3oz Marg 6oz P flour)
Spread over with
4oz sugar ⎱ creamed together
2oz Marg ⎰
add 2 eggs & mix well
add 6 tablespoons crushed
Digestive Biscuits
8oz Mixed fruit & a few cherries
Put over 325°

BRIDE'S SLICE

Ingredients:

Shortcrust pastry:
75g margarine
150g plain flour
A few spoonfuls of cold water

Filling:
100g caster sugar
50g margarine
2 eggs
6 tbs crushed digestive biscuits
200g mixed fruit
12 glacé cherries

Topping:
200g icing sugar
Water

 IT WAS BRIDE'S SLICE ALL ROUND TO CELEBRATE WITH A COUPLE WHO CAME TO ABBEY COTTAGE AFTER THEIR ROMANTIC SWEETHEART ABBEY MARRIAGE CEREMONY.

Method:

First of all, make the pastry by combining the flour and margarine, then gradually add water to form the dough. Grease a baking tray (12 x 8 inches, 30 x 20 cm) and then roll out the pastry and line the tray.

Next, make the filling by creaming together the sugar and margarine. Add the crushed digestive biscuits and the eggs to the mixture and mix well. Then, stir through the mixed fruit and cherries.

Spread the mixture evenly on top of the pastry and bake in a moderate (160°C) oven for 45 minutes.

Bring the tray out of the oven and allow to cool.

Make the icing by gradually adding small amounts of water to the icing sugar and mixing well, and spread over the cake.

Cut into 12 slices. Will keep in an airtight tin for several days.

BANANA LOAF

Ingredients:

75g butter or soft margarine
225g caster sugar
150g plain flour
1 egg
2 medium size ripe bananas
3 tablespoons milk
½ teaspoon baking powder
½ teaspoon baking soda
½ teaspoon vanilla essence

THIS IS A GREAT WAY TO USE UP OVER RIPE BANANAS!

Method:

Grease and line a loaf tin and put the oven on to 160°C.

Cream the butter and sugar together until light and fluffy. Peel and mash the bananas.

Add the baking powder and bicarbonate of soda to the flour.

Beat the egg, milk and vanilla essence together, then add gradually, mixing in with a few spoonfuls of the flour.

Finally, fold the mashed banana into the mixture.

Place the mixture into the loaf tin and bake in the oven for approximately one hour. Check from time to time. The loaf is ready when it is lightly browned and springy to touch.

Remove from the oven and allow to cool.

Remove from the tin and serve sliced with butter.

Will keep for several days in an airtight container, and can be frozen.

♥ HANDY HINT: POP OVER RIPE BANANAS IN THE FREEZER, THEN USE THEM WHEN YOU'VE GOT TIME TO BAKE

FRUIT TART LEMON
BREAD & BUTTER
PUDDING ABBEY
COTTAGE 'MURRAY
MOUND' SPONGE HOT
CHOCOLATE FUDGE
CAKE OATY APPLE
CRUMBLE CORDON BLEU
CAKE EVE'S PUDDING
PAVLOVA MERINGUE
GINGER CREAM LOG
GINGERBREAD CRISPY
APPLE CAKE

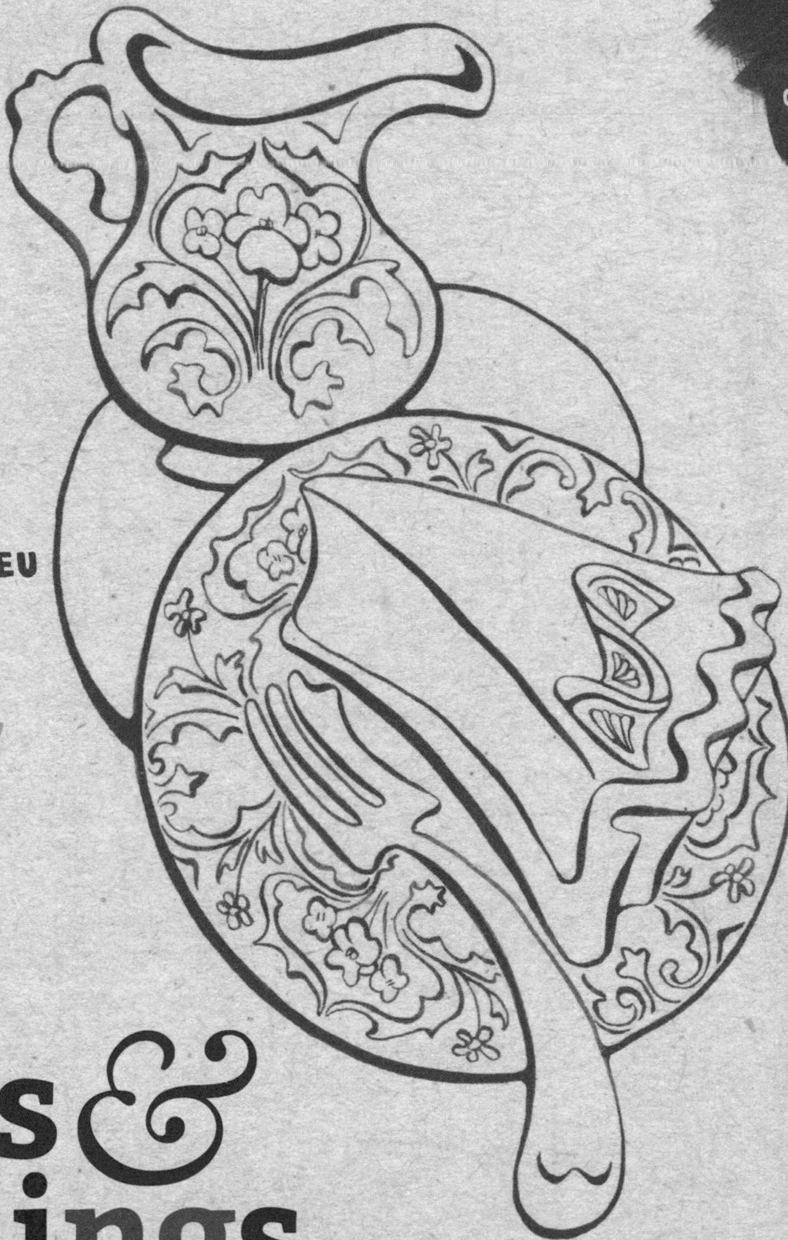

Cakes & Puddings

FRUIT TART

WILL MAKE ENOUGH PASTRY FOR 1 LARGE FRUIT TART, JUST CHOOSE WHATEVER FRUIT IS IN SEASON - RHUBARB, GOOSEBERRY THEN APPLE.....

Ingredients:

Pastry:
50g icing sugar
225g plain flour
pinch salt
75g pastry fat (eg Cookeen)
75g margarine
cold water to mix

Filling:
approximately 750g of seasonal fruit
Sugar

Method:

Pre heat the oven to 180°. This is a 'plate' tart – lightly grease a large plate.

Prepare the fruit – rhubarb will need to be cleaned and chopped, gooseberries will need to be 'topped and tailed', and apples will need to be peeled, cored and sliced. Make the pastry by placing all the ingredients except the water into a food processor and blitz until a breadcrumb like mixture is formed. Gradually add the cold water until a firm dough is formed. Turn the dough out onto a floured board and cut in two. Roll out the first piece of pastry until it is the size of the plate. Using the rolling pin, lift the pastry onto the plate.

Next, roll out the second piece of pastry to a similar size. Place the fruit and sugar on top of the first piece of pastry and wet all round the edge. Place the second piece of pastry on top, pressing the two layers of pastry together at the edges. Take a knife around the edge of the plate and trim off the excess pastry. Make a couple of cuts on the top of the pie. Brush with milk and place in the oven for 30 minutes. Serve warm with cream or Cream o'Galloway ice cream.

 CHOOSE A SEASON. SPRING, SUMMER OR AUTUMN. WILL IT BE TART OR CRUMBLE? CHOOSE YOUR FRUIT. WILL IT BE APPLES, RHUBARB, GOOSEBERRIES, BRAMBLES?

LEMON BREAD & BUTTER PUDDING

Ingredients:

1 thick sliced white loaf of bread
1 jar lemon curd
4 eggs
3 tablespoons caster sugar
275ml single cream
275ml double cream
Vanilla essence
Demerara sugar to dust

Method:

Heat the oven to 160°. Lightly grease an oven proof dish.

Butter the slices of bread and spread them with lemon curd. Cut the slices diagonally and arrange the slices of bread in the heatproof dish, overlapping each other.

Whisk the eggs and sugar with a little vanilla essence. Combine the creams, warm them gently and then stir into the egg mixture. Pour the mixture over the bread slices.

Place the dish in a roasting tray and add water to the roasting tray until it is half way up the side of the dish. Cook in the oven for 45 minutes until the custard has set and the bread browned.

Sprinkle the top with Demerara sugar before serving.

 **A PUDDING WITH A TWIST, DELICIOUSLY LEMONY**

SIT BACK AND ENJOY WHILE WATCHING WIMBLEDON

ABBEY COTTAGE 'MURRAY MOUND' SPONGE

Ingredients:

150g self raising flour
150g butter or margarine
150g castor sugar
3 eggs
Vanilla essence

To assemble and decorate:

400ml Fresh cream (whipping or double)
1 punnet of fresh Scottish Strawberries
Fresh mint leaves
Edible flower petals

Method:

Pre heat the oven to 190°C. Thoroughly grease a 25 cm savarin cake tin (to make a circular cake with a hole in the middle). Dust the greased tin with plain flour.
Cream the butter and sugar together by hand, or using a food mixer. Then gradually add the eggs and the flour. Finally add a few drops of vanilla essence.

Gently place the cake mixture into the tin and put in the oven for approximately 25 minutes. It will be ready when springy to touch.

Carefully remove the cake from the tin and leave on a wire tray to cool. While the cake is cooling, whip the cream and wash and slice the strawberries.

When the cake has cooled, slice it into two lengthwise using a sharp knife. Cover the bottom slice with half the whipped cream and sliced strawberries, and replace the top slice. Decorate the top slice with the remaining whipped cream and strawberries, and add a few sprigs of mint and sprinkle with decorative edible flower petals.

HOT CHOCOLATE FUDGE CAKE

approx 12 servings

Ingredients

Cake:

300g Self Raising flour
80g cocoa powder
185g margarine
350g caster sugar
3 eggs
2 teaspoon vanilla essence
250ml water

Fudge icing:

100g good quality cooking chocolate
100g margarine
250g icing sugar
Milk to thin

Method:

Pre heat the oven to 180°. Lightly grease and line 2 20cm cake tins.

Cream the sugar and margarine. Combine the flour and cocoa.

Add an egg, approx one third of the water, the vanilla essence and a few spoonfuls of the flour and cocoa to the creamed sugar and margarine and beat the mixture. Repeat with the remaining eggs and water until all of the flour and cocoa mixture has been used up.

Carefully spoon the mixture into the cake tins and bake the oven for about 50 mins. Remove from the oven and allow to cool.

While the cake is cooling, make the fudge icing. Place the marg and chocolate in a bowl and melt in the microwave. Add the icing sugar to the melted mixture and stir. If the icing is too thick, it can be thinned with a little bit of milk.

Assemble the cake, putting approx one third of the fudge icing in the middle, and the remainder on the top and sides of the cake.

It is lovely served slightly warm with cream or ice-cream.

- -

OATY APPLE CRUMBLE

serves 6-8

SERVE WITH CREAM OR CUSTARD

Ingredients:

Filling:

900g (approximately 5) Bramley cooking apples or mix of apples and brambles
75g caster sugar
1 teaspoon ground cinnamon (optional)

Topping:

175g butter, chopped
225g plain flour
100g demerara sugar
175g Scottish Porridge Oats

Method:

Preheat the oven to 180°C. Peel, core and slice the apples. Arrange in a large ovenproof dish and scatter the sugar and cinnamon over.

Make the topping by placing all the dry ingredients in bowl and add the chopped butter and rub together to create a crumb like consistency. Alternatively, place all the ingredients in a food processor.

Scatter the topping over the apples. Bake in the oven for 30-35 minutes until the top is golden and the apples cooked.

 DECORATE WITH STRAWBERRIES, CHERRIES OR CRYSTALLISED GINGER SERVE WITH CREAM.

CORDON BLEU CAKE

Ingredients:

Cake:
200g butter, softened
100g caster sugar
200g cream cheese
1 teaspoon lemon juice
½ teaspoon cinnamon
6 tablespoons brandy
6 tablespoons milk
30 'Nice' biscuits

Topping:
4 tablespoons caster sugar
4 tablespoons water
2 tablespoons cocoa
100g plain chocolate
50g butter

Method:

Cake:
Cream the butter and sugar together until light and fluffy. Add the cream cheese, lemon juice, and cinnamon and mix well together.

Lay out a large piece of foil on a flat surface.

Mix the brandy and milk together in a small bowl, dip the biscuits in the brandy mixture and lay them on the foil, 3 biscuits wide x 5 biscuits lengthwise.

Spread a thin layer of the cheesy mixture on top of the biscuits. Dip the remaining biscuits in the brandy mix and lay them on top of the spread.

Spread the remaining mixture down the centre row of biscuits.

Pull the foil sides lightly to make the cake into a long triangular log shape. Refrigerate overnight.

Topping:
In a saucepan melt the sugar, water, cocoa and chocolate and boil for 2 minutes. Remove from the heat and beat in the butter. Cool slightly.

Remove the foil from the cake and place on a serving dish. Brush the melted chocolate sauce over the cake. Refrigerate until time to serve. To serve, cut into slices.

EVE'S PUDDING

serves 4

Ingredients:

400g apples
Sugar to sweeten
2 eggs
100g self raising flour
100g caster sugar
100g margarine

Method:

Pre heat the oven to 180º. Lightly grease the sides of a pudding dish with butter or margarine.

Prepare the apples by peeling, chopping into quarters, removing the cores and slicing into the pudding dish. Cover with sugar.

Next, make the sponge topping by creaming together the butter and sugar. Then add the self raising flour and the eggs, beating together to get a light mixture.

Pour the sponge mixture on top of the apples and place the dish into the oven.

The pudding will require about 40 minutes in the oven and is ready when the sponge is risen and lightly browned.

Serve with custard, or with Cream o' Galloway ice cream!

CUSTARD OR CREAM? WHAT'S IT TO BE?

PAVLOVA MERINGUE

THE KIRKLAND FAMILY HAVE BEEN FRIENDS FOR MANY, MANY YEARS. ANNE WAS A WONDERFUL COOK, AND SHE VERY KINDLY SHARED HER SECRET FOR A SUCCESSFUL MERINGUE WITH MORAG BACK IN 1988. WITH THE FAMILY'S PERMISSION, WE'RE SHARING IT WITH YOU.

Ingredients:

6 egg whites
2 cups granulated sugar
2 teaspoons vanilla essence
2 teaspoons vinegar
6 dessert-spoons cold water
Pinch of salt

Method:

Pre heat the oven to 150°.

Put all the ingredients into a bowl and mix until stiff.

Grease a baking tray with cooking oil.

Take two layers of greaseproof paper and run under the cold water tap until dripping wet. Shake off the excess moisture and place the paper onto the greased tray.

Pile the mixture onto the wet paper. Do not spread, it will spread evenly during cooking.

Put into the oven for 5 minutes. Switch the oven off, and leave the meringue in the oven for 1 to 1½hours.

Serve with fresh fruit and cream.

GINGER CREAM LOG

serves 4 - 6

Ingredients:

300ml carton double cream
1 packet of ginger snap biscuits
150ml sherry (optional)
Crystallised or stem ginger to decorate

Method:

The day before:
Place half the cream in a bowl and whisk until it forms stiff peaks.

Using a long dish, use the cream to sandwich the biscuits together, forming a long roll. For a wee bit added flavour, the biscuits can be dipped in the sherry before spreading with the cream.

Cover with cling film and leave in the fridge overnight.

Next day:
Whip the remaining cream and cover the roll completely. Decorate with the small pieces of stem or crystallised ginger.

Serve immediately, cutting diagonal slices from the roll for a striped effect.

GINGERBREAD

This recipe will make a large cake, or 3 smaller loaves.

Ingredients:

250g margarine
300g black treacle (6 large spoons)
100g syrup (2 large spoons)
½ pint milk
525g plain flour
100g brown sugar
2 teaspoons mixed spice
2 teaspoons bicarb of soda
3 teaspoons of ginger
4 eggs

GINGERBREAD KEEPS WELL AND TASTES BETTER AFTER A COUPLE OF DAYS. IT ALSO FREEZES WELL.

Method:

Preheat the oven 170°. Grease and line a 23cm springform cake tin, or 3 x 2lb loaf tins.

Melt the margarine, treacle and syrup in a pan or in a bowl in the microwave. Add the milk and leave to cool.

Weigh out all the other ingredients and place in bowl, add the eggs and then the melted margarine mixture. Stir thoroughly and carefully pour the cake mixture into the tin(s).

Place in the oven. The cake will take about 1 hour 15 minutes to bake, and the loaves will be less, approximately 1 hour.

Take out of the oven and allow to cool thoroughly.

CRISPY APPLE CAKE

A DELICIOUS MOIST CAKE TO EAT ON IT'S OWN OR WITH ICE-CREAM, AND A GREAT RECIPE FOR USING UP THE AUTUMN APPLE HARVEST!

Ingredients

225g self raising flour
1 teaspoon baking powder
225g caster sugar
Sprinkle of demerara sugar
2 eggs
1 teaspoon almond essence
140g butter (melted)
400g apples, approximately (peeled and sliced)

Method

Preheat the oven to 150°.

Weigh out butter, put in a heat proof bowl and place in the oven. Grease the base and sides of a 20 cm spring form cake tin. While the oven is heating and the butter is melting, prepare the apples.

Next, put the flour, baking powder and sugar in a bowl and mix through.

Remove the butter from the oven. Beat the eggs and almond essence together, and stir this, along with melted butter, into the bowl.

Spread half the mixture into the cake tin, cover with apples, then cover with the rest of the mixture. Sprinkle demerara sugar on top.

Bake in the oven for 1 hour 15 minutes, or until nicely crusty. Set aside to cool.

Cooking With Kids

SWEETHEART
SANDWICHES
TRUFFLES FRUIT
AND BRAN LOAF
MARSHMALLOW LOG
DOUBLE CHOCOLATE
MUFFINS CHOCOLATE
NESTS PLAYDOUGH

SWEETHEART SANDWICHES

FUN SANDWICHES FOR BIRTHDAY TEAS!

makes 12 mini sandwiches

Ingredients:

6 slices white bread
Butter, or easy spread butter
Strawberry (or other red coloured) jam

Small (approximately 6cm) heart shaped pastry cutter

Method:

Remove the crusts from the bread.

Spread 3 slices of the bread with butter, and then with the jam. Put the remaining slices on top.

Using the pastry cutter, cut 4 hearts from each sandwich. You will need to alternate the cutter 'pointy bit up' and 'pointy bit down' to fit all 4 hearts out of each slice!

Also, can be made with brown bread and egg mayonnaise.

For the egg mayonnaise:
2 free range eggs
2 tablespoons mayonnaise
Salt and pepper to season

Place the eggs in a pan of water, bring to the boil and keep boiling for 8 minutes. After 8 minutes, take the pan off the heat and plunge the eggs into cold water. Leave the eggs in cold water to cool down, the remove the shells.

Chop the hard boiled eggs finely, or grate them. Place in a bowl and add the mayonnaise and stir through.

Check for seasoning and add some salt or pepper if required.

OUR WEE ONES HAVE ALWAYS LOVED MAKING TRUFFLES AS PRESENTS, AND THIS LOVELY RECIPE WAS KINDLY GIVEN TO US BY OUR LIFELONG FRIEND, LORNA

TRUFFLES

will make 36 truffles

Ingredients:

400g (large) tin of condensed milk
100g margarine
20 crushed digestive biscuits
100g desiccated coconut or chocolate vermicelli
100g drinking chocolate
Petit four cases

If the truffles are a gift for grown ups, then a wee glug of brandy or sherry can be added.

Method:

Melt the margarine with the condensed milk in a pan. Mix the crushed biscuits and hot chocolate together and then stir into melted margarine/condensed milk. Add the brandy or sherry at this stage.

Using your hands, make the mixture into small balls and roll in coconut or vermicelli. If you find that the mixture is too soft, then add a little bit more crushed biscuit.

Place each truffle in a petit four case and place on baking tray. Place in fridge until firm.

FRUIT AND BRAN LOAF

MEASURING OUT THE INGREDIENTS FOR THIS RECIPE IS GREAT FUN, NO KITCHEN SCALES REQUIRED! THERE'S NO NEED FOR A MIXER EITHER, JUST A STIR ROUND WITH A WOODEN SPOON......

Ingredients:

1 cup milk
1 cup bran breakfast cereal
1 cup dried mixed fruit
1 cup caster sugar
1 cup self-raising flour
1 medium egg beaten

Method:

Pre heat the oven to 160°. Grease and line a 2lb loaf tin.

Place the milk, bran breakfast cereal, sugar and dried mixed fruit in a bowl and leave to soak for at least an hour, or overnight.

Stir the mixture, and add the flour and the egg and mix thoroughly.

Place the mixture into the prepared loaf tin and bake in the oven for approximately 50 minutes. Check the loaf from time to time and lower the temperature if the sides are browning too quickly. The loaf is ready when it feels firm to touch.

Remove from the oven and leave to cool. This is a healthy, fat free loaf, which can be sliced and served with butter. If placed in a tin, or wrapped in cling film, this loaf will keep for several days.

- -

MARSHMALLOW LOG

BISCUITS TO BE CRUSHED, CHERRIES TO BE HALVED AND MARSHMALLOWS TO BE SNIPPED! LOTS TO KEEP LITTLE PEOPLE BUSY IN THIS RECIPE!

Ingredients:

500g of digestive biscuits
100g glacé cherries (approximately 15)
100g marshmallows (approximately 15)
400g sweetened condensed milk
25g melted margarine
25g desiccated coconut

Method:

Crush the digestive biscuits and place them in a large mixing bowl. Chop the glacé cherries in half and add to the bowl, then quarter the marshmallows and add them to the bowl (tip: use kitchen scissors dipped in water).

Finally, add the melted margarine and the sweetened condensed milk.

Stir all the ingredients together until a fudge type mixture is formed and there are no more small crumbs.

Lift the mixture onto a pastry board and form into one large or two smaller log shapes, firming with your hands.

Sprinkle the desiccated coconut onto the board and roll the log(s) in it.

Wrap the log(s) in cling fling and place on a tray in the fridge overnight. To serve, cut into slices approximately 1 cm deep.

DOUBLE CHOCOLATE MUFFINS

MUFFINS ARE GREAT FUN TO MAKE WITH TWO CHILDREN, AS THERE ARE WET AND DRY INGREDIENTS TO BE WEIGHED AND MEASURED. FOR DIFFERENT FLAVOURS, REPLACE THE COCOA POWDER WITH FLOUR, AND THE CHOCOLATE CHIPS WITH DRIED OR FRESH CHOPPED FRUIT.

will make 12 muffins

Ingredients:

120g plain flour
30g cocoa powder
85g choc chips
1 teaspoon baking powder
⅛ teaspoon bicarbonate of soda
¼ teaspoon salt
85g soft light brown sugar
85g butter
1 egg
5 tablespoon milk
1 teaspoon vanilla extract
3 tablespoon natural yogurt

Method:

Pre heat the oven to 180º.

Weigh the butter and put it in a heatproof bowl. Put the bowl in the oven to melt the butter.

Measure out the 'dry ingredients' – the flour, cocoa powder, chocolate chips, baking powder, bicarbonate of soda, salt and sugar, and place in a large bowl.

Measure out the 'wet ingredients' – the milk, vanilla, yogurt and egg into another bowl.

Remove the melted butter from the oven and leave to cool. While the butter is cooling, put paper cases into the muffin tin.

Carefully pour the butter into the 'wet ingredients' bowl and mix thoroughly. Then, add the wet ingredients to the dry ingredients and stir everything well. Spoon the mixture into the muffin cases.

Put the tray in the oven and bake in the oven for 20 minutes. Bring the muffins out and allow to cool for a few minutes before removing from the tray.

- -

CHOCOLATE NESTS

STIRRING BREAKFAST CEREAL INTO MELTED CHOCOLATE IS ALWAYS FUN! THIS RECIPE MAKES LOVELY LITTLE NESTS FOR EGGS AT EASTER TIME, OR MAYBE JELLY BEANS AT OTHER TIMES....

will make 6 nests

Ingredients:
25g margarine
25g cooking chocolate
25g caster sugar
1 tablespoon golden syrup
25g cornflakes or rice crispies
12-18 egg sweets

Method:

Put the margarine, chocolate, sugar and syrup into a pan. Put the pan onto a low heat and stir the ingredients gently until they have melted.

Turn off the heat and move the pan onto a heatproof surface. Gradually add the cornflakes or crispies and stir so that they are all covered in the chocolate mixture.

Lay out a piece of greaseproof paper. Using two spoons, create six piles of the mixture and shape them into nests with a hollow in the middle. Place the egg sweets into the nests and leave them to harden.

PLAYDOUGH

HOURS OF FUN WITH THIS HOMEMADE PLAYDOUGH!

Ingredients:

2 cups plain flour
1 cup salt
2 cups water
2 tablespoons oil
2 teaspoons cream of tartar
A few drops of food colouring

Method:

Mix all the ingredients together, then place in a pan over a moderate heat. Keep stirring and remove from the heat as soon as the mixture starts to come away from the sides of the pan and changes texture.

Tip the dough out onto a board and allow it to cool, then knead well.

Store the playdough in an airtight container.

JUST FOR PLAYING... NOT FOR EATING!

Jams & Preserves

BRAMBLE AND APPLE
JELLY SLOE GIN
RHUBARB AND ORANGE
JAM MARMALADE
STRAWBERRY JAM
GREENGAGE JAM
NANNY TED'S GREEN
TOMATO CHUTNEY

4 lbs. fruit to 3 lbs sugar

for water to boil

till set

BRAMBLE AND APPLE JELLY

GOING OUT TO PICK BRAMBLES IS A GREAT EXCUSE FOR A COUNTRYSIDE WALK IN SEPTEMBER, AND THIS JELLY ALSO USES UP SOME OF THE AUTUMN APPLES....

makes approximately 8 jars

Ingredients:

3 kg brambles (blackberries)
1 kg cooking apples
Water
Sugar

This is a two stage process, and the amount of sugar required will be determined by the volume of juice from the first stage.

First of all, wash the apples, cut into chunks and place in a large pan. Rinse the brambles and add them to the pan. Add water until the fruit is just covered. Heat the pan and boil the fruit until soft.

Next, put the contents of the pan into a jelly bag with a large bowl underneath and leave overnight.

Squeeze the bag gently to get all the juice, then discard the contents. Measure the juice into a large pan, and for every 600ml of juice, add 450g of sugar.

Heat the pan, stirring until the sugar has all dissolved. Then boil rapidly until setting point is reached.

Transfer the jelly to jars and seal.

SLOE GIN

WAIT UNTIL THE FIRST FROSTS HAVE BEEN, THEN IT'S A GREAT EXCUSE TO GET OUT FOR A WALK IN THE LATE AUTUMN SUNSHINE TO PICK SOME SLOES. THE FRUIT OF THE BLACKTHORN, YOU'LL FIND THEM GROWING IN HEDGES ALL OVER.

Ingredients:

All measurements are approximate:
1kg sloes
500g sugar
A 75cl bottle gin (or vodka)

You'll need a couple of bottles with a screwtop or stopper, and a funnel.

Method:

Wash the sloes and then prick each one with a thick needle. As you're doing this, place the pricked sloes into the bottle. You will have enough sloes when the bottle is one third full.

Next, using the funnel, pour sugar into the bottle until the bottle is two thirds full.

Finally, pour in the gin until the bottle is full and seal the bottle.

Give the bottle a gentle shake every day or so, and gradually the colour will change.

Leave the bottle for at least 3 months before straining and decanting into a clean bottle.

RHUBARB AND ORANGE JAM

RHUBARB ALWAYS SEEMS TO BE PLENTIFUL IN THE LOCAL GARDENS IN SPRING AND EARLY SUMMER AND WE MAKE LOTS OF CRUMBLES AND TARTS. THIS JAM RECIPE IS A WEE BIT DIFFERENT FROM THE USUAL RHUBARB JAM WITH THE ADDITION OF AN ORANGE.

makes approximately 8 jars

Ingredients:

4 lbs rhubarb, chopped
1 fresh orange (whole orange thinly sliced and chopped)
4 lbs sugar
1 dessert-spoon ginger

Method:

Bring all the ingredients to the boil slowly and simmer until thick.

- -

MARMALADE

LOOK OUT FOR THE SEVILLE ORANGES IN LATE JANUARY AND FEBRUARY!

makes approximately 10 jars

Ingredients:

1.35kg Seville Oranges
Juice of 2 lemons
3 litres of water
2.75kg sugar

Method:

Wash the oranges and cut each one in half. Squeeze out the juice and pips. Put the juice into the large pan, and put the pips and the pulp into a piece of muslin and tie them up.

Cut the peel and pith into thick pieces, or chop in a food processor.

Place the chopped peel, the muslin bag, the lemon juice and the water to the large pan. Heat the contents and simmer for about 2 hours until the peel has softened.

Squeeze any liquid out of the muslin bag into the pan and discard.

Now, add the sugar and cook over a low heat, stirring until the sugar has dissolved. Then, bring to the boil and keep boiling until setting point is reached.

Transfer the marmalade to the sterile jars and seal.

- -

STRAWBERRY JAM

makes approximately 8 jars

Ingredients:

2.25 kg strawberries
125ml lemon juice
2kg sugar

Method:

Wash the strawberries. Cut the larger strawberries into quarters.

Put the strawberries and lemon juice into a pan and heat gently, bringing to simmer and cooking until the strawberries are soft.

Now add the sugar and keep stirring until it has dissolved. Then bring to the boil, and boil rapidly for 15 – 20 minutes until setting point is reached. Transfer to jars and seal.

GREENGAGE JAM

THERE HAS BEEN A GREENGAGE TREE IN THE GARDEN OF ABBEY COTTAGE FOR AS LONG AS WE CAN REMEMBER. IN LATE SUMMER THE WASPS IT ATTRACTS CAN BE A BIT OF A NUISANCE, BUT WE LOVE GATHERING THE FRUIT TO MAKE SOME JAM.

ONE OF OUR GENEROUS CAIRN VALLEY NEIGHBOURS, STEVE, ALSO LETS US HELP OURSELVES TO HIS GREENGAGE CROP, AND IT'S HIS TIP WE USE FOR DEALING WITH THOSE STONES.

makes approximately 8 pots

Ingredients:

4 lb greengages
4lb sugar
½ pint of water

Method:

Clean the fruit and place in large pan with the water. Heat gently to soften the fruit. This will loosen the stones which can then be removed using a wide gauge sieve or colander.

When the stones are removed, add the sugar and bring slowly to the boil. Cook fast for 10minutes, or until the setting point is reached. Allow to cool slightly and pot.

NANNY TED'S GREEN TOMATO CHUTNEY

THIS RECIPE IS FROM SALLY AND GORDON HOOD WHO LIVED IN BEESWING. PAPA LOVED GROWING TOMATOES IN HIS GREENHOUSE, BUT INEVITABLY EVERY YEAR THERE WERE MANY THAT FAILED TO RIPEN. THIS IS NANNY'S CHUTNEY RECIPE, AND WE ALL REMEMBER BEING GIVEN A HEALTHY SERVING OF CHUTNEY WITH OUR SLICE OF GAMMON, OR IN OUR SANDWICH.

makes approximately 8 pots

Ingredients:

4 lbs green tomatoes
4 lbs cooking apples
1 lb onions
½lb sultanas
1 teaspoon salt
1 oz ground ginger
1½ oz brown sugar
1½ oz mustard seed
1 pint vinegar

Method:

Clean the tomatoes and chop roughly. Peel, core and roughly chop the apples. Chop the onions.

Place all the ingredients in a large pan and simmer gently until tender and thick. Transfer to clean, warm jars and cover securely.

THESE LITTLE PUDDINGS LOOK AND TASTE JUST GREAT!

INDIVIDUAL CHRISTMAS PUDDINGS WITH BRANDY BUTTER
PEPPERMINT CREAMS NOEL VERA MINCE PIES MIXED NUT
ROAST SAGE, LEMON AND CHESTNUT STUFFING

Seasonal Treats

Seasonal Treats

INDIVIDUAL CHRISTMAS PUDDINGS WITH BRANDY BUTTER

will make 8 individual puddings

Ingredients:

75g plain flour
1teaspoon mixed spice
½ teaspoon ground cinnamon
¼ teaspoon ground nutmeg
1 tablespoon grated lemon rind
3 tablespoons lemon juice
50g shredded suet
75g breadcrumbs
100g soft brown sugar
1 eating apple, peeled and grated
500g of mixed fruit
2 tablespoons black treacle
2 eggs beaten
350ml milk
2 - 3 tablespoon brandy
Sprigs of holly to decorate

Brandy butter:
100g butter
50g caster sugar
50g icing sugar
2 tablespoons brandy

Method:

Ahead of time:
Place all the pudding ingredients in a large bowl, then mix together to form a soft dropping consistency. Leave this mixture in fridge overnight to chill.

Make the brandy butter by beating all the ingredients together. Transfer the mixture to a serving dish and chill in the refrigerator. Next day, line 8 microwave friendly teacups with cling film and divide the mixture between them. Cover each cup loosely with cling film and pierce.

Place the puddings in a circle in the microwave oven and cook on DEFROST for 20 minutes then cook on HIGH for 5 minutes. Take care to make sure that the puddings are not over cooked as they will go hard.

Depending on the size of your microwave, it may be easier to do 4 cups at a time and give a few minutes less to cooking.

PEPPERMINT CREAMS

WHAT BETTER WAY TO END A LOVELY DINNER THAN WITH HOMEMADE MINTS! DEPENDING THE SIZE OF THE CUTTER, THIS RECIPE WILL MAKE APPROXIMATELY 36 CREAMS.

will make 36 creams

Ingredients:

2 egg whites
450g icing sugar
Few drops peppermint essence

Method:

Beat the egg whites until they are frothy. Sift the icing sugar into a bowl, then add the egg whites and the peppermint essence. Stir until a stiff dough is formed.

Dust a pastry or chopping board and a rolling pin with icing sugar. Turn the 'dough' onto the board, knead until smooth. Roll out to approximately 0.5cm thick. Using a small cutter, cut out the shapes and place them onto baking parchment dusted with icing sugar to set.

After 24 hours they can be placed in a tin, and will store for up to a month.

NOEL VERA

THIS CHRISTMAS CAKE RECIPE WAS GIVEN TO US MANY YEARS AGO BY FAMILY FRIEND VERA. IT'S DEFINITELY THE BEST CHRISTMAS CAKE WE'VE EVER TASTED. VERA'S DAUGHTER, ANNE, WAS ONE OF THE ORIGINAL TEAM WHEN ABBEY COTTAGE FIRST OPENED IN 1983.

Ingredients:

1lb self raising flour
¾ lb butter
1lb brown sugar
¼ lb glacé cherries
¼ lb lemon peel
¼ lb ground almonds
7 eggs
2½ lb Fruit (1lb currants, 1lb sultanas, ½lb raisins)
2 teaspoons nutmeg
1 teaspoon mixed spice
1 teaspoon cinnamon

Method:

Melt the butter.

Place all the other ingredients into a large bowl. Add the melted butter and stir.

Bake for 4-5 hours for the first hour at 175º, then for 3-4 hours at 150º.

Feed the cake with rum or brandy.

 IF YOU WOULD RATHER USE METRICS, JUST LOOK AT PAGE 75!

. . . .

MINCE PIES

will make approx 36 pies

Ingredients:

100g icing sugar
550g plain flour
Pinch salt
150g pastry fat (e.g. Cookeen)
150g margarine
Cold water to mix
2 jars of mincemeat
Caster sugar to dust

Method:

Pre heat the oven to 190º. Lightly grease the 12 hole tins.

Make the pastry by placing all the ingredients except the water into a food processor and blitz until a breadcrumb like mixture is formed. Gradually add the cold water until a firm dough is formed.

Turn the dough out onto a floured board and cut in two. Roll out the first half of the pastry and cut out circles with an 80mm round cutter. Line the holes in the tins with the pastry circles, gathering up the pastry off cuts and re-rolling and cutting until all the holes are lined.

Place a dessert-spoon of mincemeat in each pie. Be careful not to overfill, as the mincemeat will bubble out in cooking.

Roll out the second piece of pastry dough and cut with either a 60mm round cutter, or a Christmas shaped cutter, to make the lids. Dampen the edges of the lids with water before placing the lids on the top and pressing together to seal. Cut a wee cross in the top of each pie with a sharp knife.

Bake in the oven for 20 minutes. Remove from the oven and dust with caster sugar while the pies are still warm. The mince pies can be stored in a tin, or frozen.

MIXED NUT ROAST

Ingredients:

2 tablespoons Butter
2 garlic cloves crushed
1 large onion, chopped
50g pine nuts, toasted
75g hazelnuts, toasted
50g walnuts, ground
50g cashew nuts, ground
100g breadcrumbs
1 egg
2 tablespoons thyme, chopped
250ml vegetable stock
Salt and Pepper

Cranberry Sauce

175g fresh cranberries
100g caster sugar
300ml red wine
1 cinnamon stick

Method:

Preheat the oven to 180° and grease and line a 2 lb loaf tin.

Place the pine nuts and hazelnuts on a tray and toast in the oven. Then remove to cool. This won't take long and be careful that they don't burn.

Melt the butter in a pan and gently fry the onion and garlic for about 5 minutes, to soften.

Grind the pine nuts and hazel nuts in a food processor.

Add all of the nuts, the breadcrumbs, egg, thyme, seasoning and stock to the pan and mix thoroughly. Turn the mixture into the loaf tin and smooth the surface. Place in the middle of the oven and bake for 30minutes.

While the roast is cooking, prepare the cranberry sauce. Place all the sauce ingredients into a pan and bring to the boil. Lower the heat and simmer for 15 minutes, stirring occasionally.

Remove the nut roast from the oven and turn out of the tin. Serve with the cranberry sauce and seasonal vegetables.

SAGE, LEMON AND CHESTNUT STUFFING

OUR VERSION OF THE TRADITIONAL ACCOMPANIMENT TO THE TURKEY!

Ingredients:

Knob of butter
2 large onions finely chopped or grated
grated rind of 2 lemons plus a little juice
1 heaped tablespoon chopped fresh sage or mixed herbs
675g good quality pork sausage meat
175g to 225g roasted chestnuts peeled and chopped (or tinned)
2 eating apples peeled and grated
100g fresh breadcrumbs
2 eggs beaten
good pinch of ground mace.

Method:

Melt 25g of butter in a pan and cook the onions for a few minutes until they soften. Add lemon rind and sage, then remove from the heat and leave to cool. Transfer the onion mixture to a bowl and stir in the sausage meat, chestnuts, grated apple and breadcrumbs. Add a squeeze of lemon juice and the eggs. Season with salt and pepper and add the mace.

This stuffing can be placed in the turkey neck, and cooked with the turkey. Or, it can be cooked separately in an ovenproof dish for 30 minutes at 180°.

Working up a ~~HEARTY~~ appetite

Steeped in history, we know that New Abbey has plenty to interest visitors. There's the romance of Sweetheart Abbey and its peaceful ruins and the fascinating working Cornmill. But there's much more!

How about an interesting stroll, a more strenuous walk or a bracing wildlife walk near the coast, before rewarding yourself with a reviving bowl of soup or an afternoon tea?

On days when there's energy to burn, it's always tempting to look up at Criffel and challenge yourself to climb it. From the top the views are amazing, looking across the Solway Firth south to the Lake District fells. Or what about a walk up to the Waterloo Monument. It's a shorter walk than Criffel, and it's a steep climb in parts, but you soon forget the hard work when you clamber to the top of the memorial to take in the spectacular views over New Abbey and the Nith Estuary.

Whenever we want a short stroll, heading down from Abbey Cottage to the Cornmill is always a treat. The centre of the village is pretty and the meadow by the Pow is a lovely spot. But there is a hidden piece of tranquillity that's often overlooked, the mill pond. Sitting just above the Cornmill, you'll find it easy to pass time sitting on the bench while children enjoy feeding the ducks.

Another gentler amble can take you down from Abbey Cottage to the Cornmill by walking around the ruined, but impressive granite Abbey precinct walls. It takes you away from the road and down along the fields next to the New Abbey Pow, and gives you some lovely views back to the Abbey.

There are longer circular walks you can take too, largely on level ground. We love going to Ardwall Point and through Shambellie Woods. Check the map in the village car park for details of the routes.

Of course New Abbey's also 'on the way to the beach'. We've had at least three generations building sand castles and flying kites at Sandyhills – and hardly a school holiday passes without walks or activities at the RSPB's reserve at Mersehead. It's the kind of flat countryside that is easy walking for any age, with woodland, open areas and a long, often empty, beach that is always a big hit with the children. You'll be amazed at the sculptures they've created from the driftwood and shells.

Finally, if you fancy some modern day treasure-hunting, there are plenty of geocaches in the New Abbey and along the coast road.

Local food producers

We like to shop local, because we like to support our local businesses, and because it tastes better!

LOVELY FREE RANGE EGGS, WITH GOLDEN YELLOW YOLKS:

Mrs McMyn's Eggs
Treetops Cottage
3 Ingleston Hill
New Abbey,
DG2 8DG
Web: **mrsmcmynseggs.co.uk**
Phone: **01387 850430**

TASTY, TASTY HAGGIS & GALLOWAY BEEF

JB Houston
Greenbrae Loaning
Dumfries
DG1 3DQ
Web **www.jbhouston.co.uk**
Phone: **01387 255528**

ROAST HAM - FOR AMAZING SANDWICHES

TH Carson
The Cross
Dalbeattie
DG5 4HE
Web: **www.thcarsononline.co.uk**
Phone: **01556 610384**

AWARD WINNING CHEESES

Loch Arthur Cheese
Camphill Village Trust,
Beeswing,
Dumfries,
DG2 8JQ
Web: **www.locharthur.org.uk**
Phone: **01387 760296**

DELICIOUS HOT SMOKED SALMON & MORE

Barony Country Foods Ltd.
Carse of Ae,
Lochmaben,
Lockerbie,
Dumfriesshire,
DG11 1SE
Web: **www.baronycountryfoods.co.uk**
Phone: **01387860487**

TRULY AMAZING ICECREAM

Cream o'Galloway
Rainton Farm,
Gatehouse of Fleet,
Castle Douglas,
DG7 2DR
Web: **www.creamogalloway.co.uk**
Phone: **01557 814040**

HONEY FROM THE NITH VALLEY

Hamish Steele
Glenmidge Smiddy
Auldgirth
Dumfries
DG2 0SW
Phone: **01387 740328**

GALLOWAY WHOLEGRAIN MUSTARD, GREAT FOR HAM SANDWICHES

Galloway Lodge Preserves
High Street, Gatehouse of Fleet
DG7 2JE
Web: **www.gallowaylodge.co.uk**
Phone: **01557 814 001**

Conversions

Most of our recipes have been converted to metric measurements. The rule is don't mix metric and imperial! In some recipes we use cups, and this is a quick way of getting everything into the mixing bowl, but you might prefer to weigh out on scales, so we've included a conversion table.

CUPS	IMPERIAL	METRIC
1 cup flour	5oz	150g
1 cup caster/granulated sugar	8oz	225g
1 cup brown sugar	6oz	175g
1 cup butter/margarine/lard	8oz	225g
1 cup sultanas/raisins	7oz	200g
1 cup currants	5oz	150g

METRIC	IMPERIAL
55 ml	2 fl oz
75 ml	3 fl oz
150 ml	5 fl oz (¼ pint)
275 ml	10 fl oz (½ pint)
570 ml	1 pint
725 ml	1 ¼ pint
1 litre	1 ¾ pint
1.2 litre	2 pint
1.5 litre	2½ pint

METRIC	IMPERIAL
10 g	½ oz
20 g	¾ oz
25 g	1 oz
40 g	1½ oz
50 g	2 oz
60 g	2½ oz
75 g	3 oz
110 g	4 oz
125 g	4½ oz
150 g	5 oz
175 g	6 oz
200 g	7 oz
225 g	8 oz
250 g	9 oz
275 g	10 oz
350 g	12 oz
450 g	1 lb
700 g	1 lb 8 oz
900 g	2 lb

Index